SWOON

PHOENIX **POETS**

VICTORIA REDEL

Swoon

THE UNIVERSITY OF CHICAGO PRESS
Chicago and London

VICTORIA REDEL is the author of a previous collection of poems, *Already the World* (1995), which received the 1995 Tom and Stan Wick Prize. She is also the author of a collection of short fiction, *Where the Road Bottoms Out* (1995), and the novel *Loverboy* (2001), which received the 2001 S. Mariella Gable Award. Redel teaches in the creative writing programs at Columbia University and Sarah Lawrence College and is a member of the MFA Program in Writing faculty at Vermont College.

The University of Chicago Press, Chicago 60637
The University of Chicago Press, Ltd., London
© 2003 by Victoria Redel
All rights reserved. Published 2003
Printed in the United States of America

12 11 10 09 08 07 06 05 04 03   1 2 3 4 5

ISBN: 0-226-70612-5 (cloth)
ISBN: 0-226-70613-3 (paper)

Library of Congress Cataloging-in-Publication Data

Redel, Victoria.
  Swoon / Victoria Redel.
     p.   cm. — (Phoenix poets)
  ISBN 0-226-70612-5 (cloth : alk. paper)
  ISBN 0-226-70613-3 (pbk. : alk. paper)
  I. Title. II. Series.

PS3568 .E3443S96 2003
811′.54—dc21

                                2003047348

For Gusta Soltanitzky (1899–2002)
For every sewn dress and costume.
For Reni, Galatz, Akerman, Paris, and Constantinople.
For the stories, all of them.
And for mornings on the porch before the rest of the family woke.

Contents

Acknowledgments

Grateful acknowledgment is made to the following publications where these poems, or versions of them, originally appeared:

The Alaska Quarterly Review: "The Jumper," "Three Twelve O'clocks in a Day," "It Is Sound We're After"

Blackbird: "Swoon"

Blackbook: "Primary"

Chiron: "Marked"

Elimae (Elimae.com): "Standing Woman" appeared as "Start"

Epoch 46, no. 2: "Intentional Woman" appeared as "The Correction"; "Problem" appeared as "Math"

5_Trope (5_Trope.com): "No China" and "Where We Fuck"

Global City Review: "Another Cabin Note" and "Be So Kind"

The Harvard Review: "Such Noises" (p. 63) appeared as "Tell It"

The Laurel Review: "Where She Goes"

Open City: "The Palace of Weep"

Poetry Miscellany: "Stunt"

Prairie Schooner: "Such Noises" (p. 3), by permission of the University of Nebraska Press, 1998.

The Santa Fe Sun: "Building the Church"

Southern Indiana Review: "Hot"

StoryQuarterly 32, 1996: "Intact Woman" appeared as "Abracadabra"; "Prior Woman" appeared as "From Before I Was Born"; and "Here Is Her Detailed List"

Web del Sol (www.WebdelSol.com): "Play" and "Prior Woman"

"Tilted Woman" appeared as "Singing to Tony Bennett's Cock" in *The KGB Bar Book of Poems,* eds. David Lehman and Star Black. New York: HarperCollins, 2000.

"Tilted Woman" appearing as "Tilted Man, Tilted Woman"; "The Bounty"; "Damsels, I"; and "Intact Woman" appeared in *Poets of the New Century,* eds. Richard M. Higgerson and Roger Weingarten. Boston: David R. Godine, 2001.

"Tilted Woman" appeared as "Singing to Tony Bennett's Cock" in *Pleased to See Me: 69 Very Sexy Poems,* ed. Neil Astley. Northhumberland, UK: Bloodaxe Books, 2002.

*

Much gratitude and love to Bill Hayward, Marie Howe, David Dodd Lee, Donna Masini, Jason Shinder, David Wojahn, Maggie Anderson, Tom Sleigh, and the Writing Program at Vermont College Community for their suggestions and encouragement on versions of poems and the manuscript. All thanks to Bill Clegg and Randy Petilos. And always I am indebted to my father, Claudia, Bill, Jonah, Gabriel, Jessica, and a lifetime of friendship with strong, passionate, funny, loving, smart, beautiful women.

Such Noises

Akhmatova said that I was wrong.

She scolded me to get off the lily pad
with its tethered sway, its crushed, show-off bloom.

I looked around, waiting for the melody makers.

She berated me like every Russian woman,
which is to say she sounded like my mothers.
Am I right or am I wrong? says one who stitched my hem.
I have the sixth sense, says one who poured me juice.

With what shame I sank off the lily pad
and swam to her on the muddy, littered bank.

Akhmatova gave me no chances.
Wake up, girl, she says, wagging at me my own strappy sandals.

I listened again for the melody makers,
while Akhmatova touched the wronged skin of my hips.

Such noises I heard then, noises to wither my creamed and polished heart.

Somewhere in the Glorious

Anyway here I am somewhere smack in the Glorious
where every station has a wannabe lover.
I'm going deep in the human bible.
Ready or not, Graceland, bend into the microphone.
      I am all melting.
Feel the heat? Behold the dreamer cometh,
and comes, always,   too late,   too fast,   days,   nights
on the express, a rim of black dye staining his pale neck.
If it's the nighttime, best not look straight into the moon.
If it's the daytime, deliver me from this muddy Nashville
where a boy drinks cups of water and gargles Home On The Range.
      Kiss me wetly with your heated lips.
I have only all my waiting. For what have I waited
by cross street and elbow, for what gadget of transformation?
Did I once look up to see a large and arbitrary nude?
It did not waltz or stumble, but inching made its way
by cradle, by waddle right past me.
What wild animal went where?
Let me admit, I dissolve feverish for anything.
If this were a smell, let it be rust.
Let there be in somewhere other than now
a color called his sticks and stones.
I'm everyone's fool. I'm ready to understand
that the Glorious will not have me in my present state,
will not rock through to see where I have waded.
Here there is a daytime and a nighttime and a runaway local.

Look for the blurry redemption, whizzing past stations, every stop
a preparation through which I have moved too quickly.
Did I think twice that I could have everything?
Here the prong-horned antelope appears on a hill,
watches, waits, turns, gores or does not, and is gone.

And So I Went

And so I went to a place I had waited for.
The loosestrife was a high purple screen.

The loosestrife in a certain light looked red.

In that place everything blue flies.
The dragonflies in coupled blue electric flight.
The great blue heron scares up, leggy and long necked.
The spider in her suspension strung out from the dock to where?

I wasn't sure I knew how to be there without my worry.
I tried to take the mantle back;

my list of what needed me fell from my pocket.

  The loosestrife in a certain light looked like a high burnt wall.

Cabin Note

We are still waiting.
    But for what?

The sun to come out.   The sun comes out.
The wet wood to burn hot.   The stone cabin to heat up.
        You to come closer.

What we do we do in this life with our clothes still mostly on.

Damsels, I

Not for pleasure alone do I pleasure
standing in a dark corner of our home
leaning into your hand fuck
while in their room the children toss in sleep.

If not for paradise then for what
do I rut, incorrigible in the palm of your hand?

Damsels I have been, in waiting, larcenous
all my olden days ago, the one of me righted
to never love, the other of me clasped entirely in attendance.

Now is she whole parceled in me.

Now brilliant pleasure, in truthe, in soule, in hearte, verily.
What is true manifests truly against my ancient thieving topology.

No China

Kneel on the floor. Cut the last late summer tomatoes, peppers,
    slit the thick fennel bulb.
Plastic forks left from yesterday's Chinese lunch.

How many days in this room without even a proper bed?

We outgrow everything too quickly.
No China could contain us.

Come eat, so that we get on with our hungers.

Swoon

There they were!
under tops made—I'm not sure of what—
a bit of tissue, a sheerest stretch of gauze, filament.
They roamed sheathed in triangles
fixed like Band-Aids.
I alarmed myself.
How I wanted to heft and pet and handle.

It was like those first fall days at school
—the one I recall, Celeste,
back from her summer was breasted—suddenly,
entirely—her whole body
a shout under a ribbed blue sweater,
as if she'd written a punch line
or bought the getup at a tourist roadstand.
It didn't matter who she'd ever even been before.
At night in front of bedroom mirrors,
it was Celeste we searched out,
looking for the nub of what she'd become.

But today, outdoors—the young women—
and I was short of breath.
The whole street tinseled in the quick spring air.

The sound as they wisped past. I was unhinged.
As if they had just invented breasts!
What I might do.
What I might never do in a life,
and then, still, husband, my life be done.

Where We Fuck

Now, suddenly, out of nowhere, Düsseldorf.
Suddenly now, nowhere but German towns
where you rise from a cot in the Hotel Garni.

It starts with a deceptively blue sky.

Here it is hot and getting hotter.
German towns where you walk twisted, stone streets.

Already I am thinking Potsdam. Do the streets twist?
And in Berlin? Do they lead

back past the hotel clerk who lets the phone just ring?
I would love you in any city. Before in damp Dublin.

Rome could be Hoboken. Your body on any bed.
Or now between cities where you are edged at evening.

You are street and canal and blind alley.
You are station, car lot, and steps to the palace.

The sky is our thick body. Rub way in. Come out all red.

Building the Church

Here in this Venice,
we are Marco Polo.

Taste of coriander, bright
pepper, melon, the musky

heart of artichoke. Oh—
to the delicacy of such East!

We follow the Law.
Carrying home on flung vessels

Greek horses, alabaster,
veined marble, clay,

the scrawled hieroglyphs
tacked in distant phone booths.

We carry home fragments
to build our watery church.

Here we plunge to surface divine.

Hallelujah Jam

What decoy praise is this night,
Sunday at a West Side dive
where nothing's left of Saturday's mix
but the guy scraping air guitar to Layla's riff
and the girl yanking off
her boyfriend's Bill Clinton mask.

Glory them in the misfit light—
they're pals, our buds tonight
kind enough not to stare
at our middle-aged rocker's groove,
hip to hip, we're stunning
runaways, blocks from the bus terminal.

If weeks from now there's almost nothing
left of us but old neighborhoods
where walking down the street we'll face ourselves,
then let others go after the shifting moon
or croon for the distant stars
on their wobbled axis.

Let for us the eternity jukebox play it again—
this hallelujah jam in love
with midnight doorways, the imprint

of your face knocked up close to mine.
Praise the human pulse, praise joy, baby,
a shake-it dance floor. Praise praise.
Praise it. Truth. Come closer.

Steerage

I wake in water. My love wakes too.
We dry off to wet again.

We boat in our bath up rivers to ports of fragrance.
We lily. We petal and polish and tart.

Courtesan, courtier, my primped up velvet cushion,
my rose, that brilliant harlot, a crimson shirt sashed up on him.

We buff and perk each other's cheeks.
My love goes this way. Out into the cloudy sea.

Look, Love. Do you see?
We prepare all day for night.

Pavane

Obviously this is not a painting but the color of butter,

blond and flesh like any ooh la la in the Palais Royale.

I dream a lot in the tub.   Who wouldn't?   In here it is a jamboree.
In here we smell of lake water.   Wrapped in gowns of foil and grass.
We hem ourselves against shores of skin.

We go gorgeous.

The Marquis, the Marais, or the whole thing. Who wouldn't take warning in
      your fingers?
Love, baby, beauty is no show, but I'm peeking anyway.
I promise anyone anything if I get to dance. I sew my fingers with nylon
      thread.

If you hear water now, you're wrong.

Listen to the Marquis.   Get out !   Go!   The poor human body turns out to
      be clairvoyant.
They're ready to chop off your too long neck.

This Is the Dream of Margaret Meadows

Not her dream, but yours,
a pattering that backs into you now,
her small feet receding,
the weedy flourish of her hair,
yards and yards and
she is always tangled and running

down the ripped-up street of your dreams,
chasing another kid's runaway pet.
She is five and grumpy with hunger.
She turns and waves.
She comes to you wavering
on saddle shoes that spring to stilettos.
You would like more silky nights
of this but she is whining, ready

to trip into another dreamland.
She is the girl-next-door to a house you can't remember.

The town keeps no record that you left.
Driving through it again
—almost accidentally—
stopping at curbs and houses, saying to yourself,
this is where I first . . . .

pointing out the music shop
where you worked your lip on a rented horn.

But the whole place makes you silly,
bruised by strip malls where there should be the fields
you walked through in a haze of wishing your way out.
Here, erections are missing, or . . . Or what?
Don't start in with somebody else's fast language.
There's nothing missing,
or years later, the street's dug up,
new macadam rolled down, sparkly at night.

Give us Margaret buried in your mulched heart.
And Margaret, now, always five, is still running.
She is frantic and ravishing and refusing to sleep
in some dream where she never intended to mean anything.

Give us the grace of her disheveled narcissus,
her flowering in dinner light. She is here
touching your feet, glorious. We are she
not shied by chubby girl fingers.
Once you were five. Now you are fifty.
How will you find her when town is rezoned,
after you've learned that the real secret
isn't even in the picture, won't enter the dream
until the intersection, you know the one.

Sail Well Like This, Hurry

When the flat garbage boat weighs past, heavy with elaborate holdings,
I do not hold my breath and ask forgiveness for us in the alabaster palace.
Still, I have seen red and gold threads around a girl's throat and it has stung
    my eyes with all the wanting.

Please know, I endeavored to forget no one. The cook, the potter, the butcher,
    the overseer.
Small and large, our preparations are a dusty business.

Today I watched a convoy of sailing ships.
Their hulls might have been made of paper, they looked so brief.
You cannot imagine what I have seen. On one a wigged man stripped bare his
    own scalp. On another a kneeling captive sang of rain.
I have seen the height of the annual floods.
There is reason for concern.

Beloved, you must know I am always hurt considering the red thread.

Be So Kind

My sisters and I belong in the Russian story where plump dark bread is clothed
    and saved each night.

There is the porcelain bowl one sister weeps into and washes red stockings.
In the courtyard where the other sister hangs her embroidered linens,
    you can smell the river Prut.
I am tutored for examinations but leave the University to nurse a trembling
    uncle.

At night we button our hands to silk blankets.

When the betrayals begin, we paint ourselves and nest inside one another.

Here we totter unfit for your America. We kneel, fingers stuck in our throats.

Please, be so kind as to let the author know: if there is any choice in the matter,
    my sisters and I,
we'd rather kill each other in our Bessarabian woods where snow mounts
    indecently to the top branches.

Stunt

If you want to watch me lie then watch me
tell you this isn't me, circa 1982,
taking a hitch with the Derby Crash & Stunt Car Wonder Boys,
their bus rigged wonderfully with bunks
so they can cool between gigs
trying to calm off whatever speed they're throttled on.
Or just climb aboard to see how the stunt cars look,
hitched up and stacked on a carrier,
stenciled letters polished on red, dented hoods
so WONDER BOYS ripples its own trippy sanity.
Maybe you can see that I've already done the inside-out trick
down one side of Nova Scotia's coast,
the bus rocking steeply near Cape Breton
where I'm hoping to catch up with my other half.
The villages we pass are clutters of houses
pinned together by painted wooden butterflies.
Sure, the Wonder Boys try to peddle off something
they swear will make me holy and flip and unbreakable.
But soon they've crashed, cranky, lost boys,
and I become Wendy, twisting through the bus,
ready to sing about home and the boys going weepy
for everything that wasn't in any Neverland.
The route curves into noon.
High on nothing but the rollick, I cut the driver lines
while he grumbles *Stairway to Heaven.*
He could let me off near their fairgrounds,

but won't I stay for the show? watch the boys?
even spin myself once around the track?
Maybe by now you want to beg me to get out,
stretch your legs, turn up smiling in the picture postcard.
But just then I see butterflies break from houses,
all the Painted Lady monarchs—
each with her 10,000 eyes, her own 3-week, 1000-mile life—
hover then plunge into the Sound.
If this is a joyride, it's close to ending and I can't stop.
I'm making my own breakneck record,
racing on the wheelie of my own shadow.
Later, with a man who bricks his backseat
with loaves of stale bread, I wave past Halifax.
By summer's end, my only happy friend
is zapped by lightning on a no-cloud day.
Then mother strokes again and is dead.
I pray you've had enough
of your own one life to know truth from a trick.
Look at me go and, dearest Future, believe that,
within a year, the rest of what I was was gone.

Hot

        How
it used to be is me out driving
always spotting something burning on the flats below the Jersey Palisades.
        How it used to be
is a race of worry, water bottled and stored in the trunk.
Houses? Factories? A car shop made of wood,
trapped men in greasy flammables.
        No one
else on the road looked west,
where raised flames waved to me for help.
The river between did not matter.
The flashing sirens close by did not matter.
I needed to hold up
each tilted Palisade column, save every workingman.
        How it is now
is my car junked on the street and hours in your arms.
I wake to find the city
corded with yellow tape,
gloved officers putting spent shells into plastic bags.
When I slip by flinty with our sex,
everything ignites.
        Let New Jersey burn.

Frontier

Sweet the heart, sweetheart,
the way we go on, unbeaten,
even now old, unmended gates where tilted carts
pass through, not retreating, junked
high with the family plates and clock,
the wares to pawn or save for passing on.

Night's not easy for travel.
The fox beneath the bridge,
the weasel sucking dry farm hens,
there's always border guards. I tell you,
gully, city block or treeless ridge,
or wheels careening out in the open,
there's no simple passage, no guarantee
that once we're there, there's safety.

Call it foolhardy, call it
not worth a pan of fool's gold this quest,
this heart's expansion, unterritorial,
no claim for land rights or birth,
no rivalry east or west, just, sweetheart,
a glory all this chance to live, all the self alive,
not hitched to outpost settlements,
not even horses driven, but the drive.

Marked

I sat on a blanket while he fished. When I said my need, he dug a large hole
  in the sand
where I could squat to shit and still watch the sea.

I was bloated and full to empty. For cleaning there was water and the sea's
  pebbled bottom.

I covered the hole in with sand. He marked the place with large rocks.

You who know me know I was happy.

Another Cabin Note

Even now the fear that this has happened before.
Of course there were bodies.   And you inside other bodies.

But the entering.   And after you have gone in,

the going in.

Such Noises

The boys say they get it, how it's not them, exactly.

The boys say the fish lives at Dad's.

The boys say it's okay to become girls in one poem. But only one poem, okay.

The boys say you owe us a quarter for each of the swearwords.

The boys say who exactly was Jean Lafitte?

The boys say why did we ever go to that beach?

The boys say will there be a sequel?

The Palace of Weep

Take that I am afraid of how Goya saw the world.
Take that I love Goya and his dark invention of my life.

My life is the invention of all women waiting on West Side stoops,
happy for an iced coffee before picking up kids.

I cannot sleep at night for the chimney sweeps who live in Blake.
Blake and Goya ignite in this city's children their doses of asthma, plastic prizes
for cindered bronchia, the chemical twitch and Ritalin fretting.

I think I have everything except keys which I am always losing.
I have the squashed hope of every showy failure before us.
The signs on cars plead our criminal efforts: *trust me I have nothing.*
When a siren stops in this city, people worry.

Take my hope for the palace of the unconverted, the stumbled
offers of the confused, the stalled recovery of each morning
but not the Freon steam cleaning another hole in our thin universe.

This is 79th Street where wind is our hero.

Take the double-parked, GOLDEN KEY 580-0066,
24-Hour Emergency Service. Take the locksmith
who walks—belts, tools, and a chalky, damp jumpsuit—
straight through an afterschool melee of mothers and children.

Let's drift together up the tipsy raft of Broadway
bannered with the bedazzled prayers of every generation.
Leave for a next true world the boy who runs
out of school and up into my arms.

I want more Goya. I want more July. "I want my mother,"
moans a little girl. So the boy answers, "It's okay. You can share mine."

Boy Food Man

All night the boy is hungry, looking up crumb-faced saying, I need food.
And the mother? —she follows through the house
with fruit and Jell-O, toasted rolls, plates of sliced leftovers,
saying, Do I look like a restaurant? She's pouring milk
and pouring juice, and after a last plate of crackers by his bed,
he wanders to the kitchen saying, I'm too hungry to sleep.
You're full, the mother says, too full for sleep,
so the boy comes in close, rubbing against the mother by the sink
saying, Please? Can't you see I'm growing? Of course she sees it.
How can she avoid it? The way day-to-day pants scooch
higher up his legs or how he's taken to walking staring down
as if his own too big feet will trip him, which they do,
all shuffle and underfoot, everything a knock, a shatter in her house,
dishes he drops and the mother finds him half asleep licking a spoon.
What are you doing? she asks, but she can see
he's more than half asleep, he's in a drift.
If she gets him upright he wants her to lift him
but she can't carry a thing so big as the boy
he's gone and stretched himself into. It's not my fault,
he says and though she says, I know, guiding this little man to bed,
doesn't she more than a little think it is his fault!
—this hunger that will not stop, as if he made a choice to let his body thicken.
She's seen him inspecting at the hall mirror the wider shoulders,
there's even—it seems too early—a stain of hair above his lip.
Everything he wants to be is older, bedtime, new words
she hears him trying out. She's not prepared.

Tucked in, he starts to ask, Can I have one last . . .
she cuts him off, snaps, No! He's a huff and pout, practically in tears.
He whines, All I wanted was a kiss. She's quick to lean in—he's just a child—
but he holds on, fixed, hugging hard.
Watch out! He has to eat through her to pass on.
Arms clasped tight, he'd gobble her up to make the weight
of his affection too much for only her to bear.

Stridor

This time when my son's best friend Ernie comes over to our house he does
    not die
when he says, "I don't like Willy Wonka Gobstoppers," tosses one
    in his mouth and chokes.

Would you have known that the caught, gurgling sounds as he lurches
    through rooms,
heaving his narrow body in jerks as if to pop the candy free from his
    own throat,
indicate air—not much air—but some, enough that he turns white, green,
    but not blue
as I fist short jabs to try and force the bit from wherever it's lodged and
    won't come out
by my hand or the other mother's hand or the babysitter's hand?

Or would you know we're out of trouble when the Emergency Vehicle
    Technician clamps oxygen over his mouth,
calls: *child in stridor* over the radio: *child in stridor,*

later admitting that it is her son she imagines working on,
the metal bits she swipes from his baby mouth, the handfuls of unchewed
    shoved food,
everything dangerous, oversized, and electric,
and the safe dangerous too, the way his own sleepclothes could kill him,
or his thumb, or these streets of men who, just safe from boyhood,
carve themselves and eat themselves and throw themselves into death

as if into the arms of ready mothers?

So hearing the ping of it uncaught against the vehicle's metal floor,
which of us is prepared to take a certain breath? We hear the rolling of it.
Who is ready to boast about living to the living.

August

"That's lucky," says the woman at the rainy beach when I say he is not
    their father.

We both hang back against the cars watching like some shared, drizzly destiny
the poncho-men cast lines halfheartedly. My boys, already tangled in fishing
    tackle,
frisk the shoreline, baiting waves with swings of frozen squid.

Lucky is what luck will have— "Please," she says, "a man at all."
Or that what comes to us comes fretful and rogue and waves back
to where I stand with a woman who hurries to tell me in one breath details
of a life she would not want me to repeat.

I will only say she never intended any of it.

Here's luck again, a squall of weather driving them ragtag up to the parking lot,
    unhooked,
fishless, ready to be fed.

The Bounty

Dear Jerry,
      While you and your Pittsburgh buddy,
the venerable Jack Gilbert, read to poets gathered in that same city,
I was walking the aisles of Costco with Jonah and Gabriel.
Have you ever been there, or in one of these warehouse food chains,
stores of the Alice-eat-me variety, everything enlarged, larger than life,
at least my life with its city cupboards, but, also, stores where my all-American
—albeit first generation—appetite for purchase
is born and born again in the next aisle where a forklift pulls out a crate
      of Dunkaroos?
The boys scream for everything big.
You, with grown children, what do you know from Dunkaroos?
And my God, the austere Jack Gilbert.
What would Gilbert think of the double-sized cart overfilled with thirty-six rolls
      of Charmin,
bulk-wrapped Bounty, twelve for eight dollars and seventy-nine cents, and cases
      of Juicy-Juice juice boxes?
Food chains with not a thing in my cart from the food chain.
But you understand, Jerry, the deals, Jerry, the deals.
Gilbert, with his mountain and his poem "Hunger" that I read to students
to take them to the line, "going beyond the seeds,"
what would Gilbert think of Jonah and me filling to overflowing the oversized cart,
and Gabriel piled high in the cart, holding a two and one-half pound box
      of cheddar goldfish.
Did he read the poem "Hunger"? Did you read your song of the green willow?
Or was it all new poems and in your hometown, too.

I would have liked that, too, to be childless in Pittsburgh, among poets, even with
    my shyness of poets.
Instead, there was enough French's Mustard to squirt the boys through childhood.
But the deals, Jerry, and I have the receipt to prove it.
That's thirty-six rolls of toilet paper at twenty-four cents a roll and the twelve for eight
dollars and seventy-nine cents comes to seventy-three cents a roll of paper towels
    and so on up to two hundred eighty-eight dollars and fifty-seven cents.
With not a vegetable or fruit in the cart.
I remember my first time, not at Costco but at BJ's,
which is the same but with a different name.
Jonah, maybe just two months, woke with a raucous hunger.
I nursed sitting on stacked crates below the stocked warehouse shelves.
The shoppers gave me terrible looks. I tried to write a BJ's poem
but got stuck with a fake Whitman love of the things
and a true highbrow hatred of glut without even a mention of
    Jonah's delicious suck.
This time there was also a frenzy of sucking,
the kids wanting to eat and drink everything in the car
and both boys screaming, "There's nothing at all here to eat!"
What's left? I got lost on 95, brought Jonah late to his violin lesson.
Waited out front with Gabe asleep in back.
That's when I had the chance to think of Pittsburgh, of poems, of you
    and your friend.
Imagine Jonah with his quarter-size violin. Imagine Dunkaroos.
His small fingers, his wrist held just right to bow.
The bounty of your music. Gilbert's strict beauty. Gabe sleeping
    through it.
And this, my happiness, Jerry, the whole heartbreaking deal.

Bedecked

Tell me it's wrong the scarlet nails my son sports or the toy store rings he clusters
      four jewels to each finger.

He's bedecked. I see the other mothers looking at the star choker, the rhinestone
      strand he fastens over a sock.
Sometimes I help him find sparkle clip-ons when he says sticker earrings
      look too fake.

Tell me I should teach him it's wrong to love the glitter that a boy's only a boy
      who'd love a truck with a remote that revs,
battery slamming into corners or Hot Wheels loop-de-looping off tracks
      into the tub.

Then tell me it's fine—really—maybe even a good thing—a boy who's got some girl
      to him,
and I'm right for the days he wears a pink shirt on the seesaw in the park.

Tell me what you need to tell me but keep far away from my son who still loves
      a beautiful thing not for what it means—
this way or that—but for the way facets set off prisms and prisms spin up
      everywhere
and from his own jeweled body he's cast rainbows—made every shining true color.

Now try to tell me—man or woman—your heart was ever once that brave.

A Roving

Now the boy loves everything pirate.
No, now he is a pirate for weeks, then months,
a year with two belts crossed across his shirt,
his shorts less shorts than fringe.
And if his mother forces shoes, then it's only red snowboots
he'll deign to wear to the park in June. He has no time for grown-ups
who joke at his seaworthy name. Did Red Mulligan
or Jean Lafitte put up with such mockery without at least a bit of blood?
Buccaneer and pirate, he's not above a taste for cruelty
but he's not the Frenchman l'Ollonois who cut the heart
from a Spanish prisoner and ate it on the spot.
Among the playground fools, he's a castaway, cast ashore
he's planning to nab a vessel, captain it,
take along his mother as his first and only mate.
She'll do, he says, even without the wooden leg.
The pile of dinner bones mark treasure,
his chance to haul up a sunken chest of dubloons.
All he wants are clues and maps.
By December, he promises, they'll capture an island.
At night he sends his mother up the crow's nest.
She watches down on the tossing compass of his sleep,
his setting out for zones torrid, equatorial,
the needle of his body adjusted against the truer north.
Too soon, she knows, he'll give up roving, join the ranks,

live by leagues of fellowship. And the mother?
She's waiting for the Caribbean,
loving the rogue before he was swallowed whole.

Primary

An economist, an arbiter of labor disputes, "And now," she tells me, "now just a full-time mother," sits under an umbrella on the beach.

Her umbrella is red and yellow and blue and below it her brown skin shines darkly with the stripes of primary colors. "Maybe, before I lose my entire mind," she says touching her stomach which has the helmeted shape of the next baby, "I think I better take myself back to school and learn again to think."

I tell her part of what I know.

That we are at the dinner table, my husband and friends eating the food I cooked while the baby slept. Or, they eat and talk and drink and talk, my husband and the friends and where am I? I am holding up the floorboards under the dinner table set directly above the baby's crib. "What do you think?" they ask me. I cannot follow the conversation. I am too busy. I hover. I float above the crib. I crawl inside the crib and dream that I hold the ceiling up.

Her child pours the sand over his head then starts to cry. "Now, now, silly bird," she says, brushing sand out from where it sticks in the child's eyes and mouth.

This is my new job, my official calling. I find the new mothers and tell them that when I woke from the dream there were more dinners and always floorboards of unproven strength.

Here is the other part of what I know.

The red and the yellow make orange.

The blue and the yellow make green.

The red and the blue make purple.

That is all. Those are the combinations. Perhaps other mixtures are up for grabs.

It is industry. It is labor.

Play

Today my happiness is like my friend's infant son napping in the stroller.
"He's been sleeping for so long," she says, "and what the royal bitch is,
he'll be up all night raring to go." But now he's in it,
sleeping hard despite the way she nudges him, wipes his damp hair,
nibbles flushed cheeks, saying, "Hey up, Sleepy, you're missing all the fun."
He brushes against her poking hand with his hand but doesn't wake.
Slump-fitted in his stroller, his neck cricked at some quirky angle,
cranked forward, he looks like he can't be comfortable that way,
or even after she's dragged him up, his dangle body slouched against the chair
of her body and he's still all shudder, he's grunty breath and snore,
some spit he babbles while she jiggles him and his eyelids twitch,
lifting to show a flutter of white.
And my friend, who called me up to say, "Please, just meet me. I need to talk."
can barely talk with me at all, she's so beside herself,
frantic, really, begging, poking him awake.
But can he wake to please her whom more than anyone he loves to please?
Even if somewhere in that sleeping head he hears her pleading,
"Don't you think you've slept enough?"
he can't pull up to join her or, if he woke, have the words
to say that it's not for good or bad the body sleeps,
but because, like happiness, unruly given any given day,
it's what exactly the body, despite all reason, needs.
Then, just as suddenly, he startles, crying, asleep, then eyes blinked open,
though not so much awake as stunned,
my friend trying to contain his jerky thrusts, trapping
his stiff flailing arms inside her arms,

shoots me a tell-me-what's-next? look while she rocks him,
repeating, " I'm here. I'm here, my Love."
And my skittery happiness takes off on action wheels that stutter,
then zoom into traffic. Look at me!
I've so little to tell my friend that makes any sense at all.
Can we meet again tomorrow? Look for me!
I'll be there crashed against my own sharp corners.

Wrong

Today I have been the difficult child,
have yanked, whining, no! no! no! Insisted
that this minute every jacket already be zipped.
Every crayon this day was dropped against me.

In tantrum, enraged, I raged the last forkful be a grateful bite.
Every word, a shout until, finally, I threw it down
and on the street before the good, passing citizens,
slapped the child, screaming "I'm the parent!"

Now the bad child I am is shut up,
sulking in her room, waiting for a parent's stiff voice to soothe.
Out there, the real child marches, flushed,
righteous, stroking his wounded cheek.

Smells victory. Wants a medal. Won't give an inch.

Problem

The two boys win three fish at the end of the summer fair. The one boy names his two fish Buddy and Malcolm and the other boy names his one fish Fred. By the time the boys get home with the three fish, fill a soup bowl with water, Fred, they decide, is sick and needs an immediate operation which leaves him one hundred percent dead. But the boys keep cutting him up in the interests of science, slitting out what they say is intestines, carving out a tiny black eye which gets left on the table while they toast bread for fish food to feed the remaining two fish, Buddy and Malcolm. Some time later, Buddy dies when no one is watching which leaves only Malcolm who, by now, moved to a real fishbowl with a shake a day of real fish food, lives on for many months on into and right through the fall without showing any sign of being a weak goldfish from a summer fair. One boy, in winter, wakes in the night, "Fred is dead," he weeps to his mother. "And he has no eyes left to find his two brothers or to make his way home in the dark."

Round

Who wakes cold started?
Heart bleating, bah bah—
Not a sheep to count—

Sons asleep, the stuttering ones—
A messy runted litter
of nonsense wool.

Who wakes wooly hearted?
Who skitters through the night?
Whose heart—bahs—a sheepish mess?

Whose mess?
Whose sleeping litter
Unbeds me?

Unbedded messy heart!
Nonsense skitters!
Bah bah stutters!

The cold sons count!
The sheepish litter!
Not asleep!

Such wool!

Bright Hill

To look at my friend's daughter
in the white clip light of the x-ray machine,
she's only half alive, the right brain dark,
inactive, no synaptic rendezvous

just odd misfiring, enough seizure
activity to worry doctors, no language,
no chance that she will be this child
I watch in her third June, blaze up the bright hill

with the other daughters and sons
to play out intricacies they devise.
My friend says it still comes over her,
driving home from work, enough dread,

exhaustion already spent for a lifetime
of splints and braces, the eye-patches this girl
throws off in a wake behind her, the ways a mother
has to be happy to watch her daughter run at all,

then run a limping zigzag path and always last in line.
By nightfall she's our honest winner, her jar jammed
with the brightest snap of firefly, and the older kids
pouting, "It's not fair," and "Go on, count them."

What's fair in the folds of the mind? What lost spark
is reinvented so that in the instrument dark, in
the sonogram's gauge and measure,
there is no number that accounts for rampant love

or the way a child works against clamped muscles,
talking her stunted hand open, opposing its own clenched will.
What's fair is that we know so little of the mind.
Not only the turns of phrase turned meanly against ourselves,

but the divagations and unruly hope, the way a child
believes that if he could only learn to whistle
he'd spend a whole day whistling.
The way an x-ray tells only one story about a girl.

Carrying in picked-over dinner plates,
we are fretting mothers, someone's brother's friend
knows of a new operation. We bargain over the incalculable.
"Hey, look. Look at us!" the kids shout.

While outside, in the summer garden, robber
chickens peck and sneak. By September
eruptions of wild sweet lettuce spread frill
and heady among the rinded, shining melons.

Stop It

The woman stands in the hallway shrieking like someone else's ridiculous
     mother.

What could be so terrible? —dawdling? forgetting again to brush teeth?
The children, stunned, look up from untied shoes.
She's caught in the plain light. Caught in the ordinary light.
What's the solace? That they go off to school? That in the other ridiculous
     homes,
the other women tremble.

Who is not beside herself? Who is not trying to remember how to speak?

Where She Goes

After he takes them for his Sunday and she is alone,
free, the envy of the married mothers,

the envy of herself all the fetch-them-home-
from-school days of the week—she rides the train

down to stores lazy with out-till-dawn girls
who call her Honey. She lets them dress her up.

These never-sleep girls declare her fierce
in a satin halter and pants. I'm someone's mother, she says,

holding up softened breasts. Don't even tell us, they say zipping
her into something once all too alive.

It's one o'clock. She does what they tell her.
There are five hours left.

She waits all day to call the kids to say good night.

The Jumper

Of course he was fat. Wore glasses.
Pants, etcetera. Shoes, etcetera.
He was everything etcetera, up to the snot

that burbled out his nose when they stood him
on the bridge to make him jump
into the shallow, fetid, littered, mud-thick water.

He was so like the boy
you'd make jump, it wasn't funny,
but, of course, it was and, when he did it,

he was the textbook boy jumping.
It took time, the jumping, which he did,
though it was less a jump than a resignation,

a yielding of his body to its rightful use.
It took some time, too, the getting out,
thick mud, waddle, etcetera,

wrappers stuck like name tags on his shirt.
I want now to remember his name, because,
though I know it can't be this way, the way

I hear it now, twenty years later, my sons
having banded to gang against a neighbor kid,
the children all stand on the bank chanting

his name in that first warm seeded day,
a name so astonishingly familiar,
like a right answer, I hear it, close to me,
cribbed, exactly my own.

It Is Sound We're After

Up an abrupt, rutted, muddy hill to the violin maker's shop,
I tell my son that it matters that it's hard getting to a room
so flooded with shear, undusty light we squinch our eyes
to see the stacked and numbered planks of Vermont maple

he ages ten years before they're joined and cut.
Then he roughs, gouges the insides, waits again,
a month at least, to note the wood's play and warp.
It is sound we're after with bird's-eye bottoms, tops of spruce.

What mother would not want to stand among the sounds Vivaldi urged
from his orphaned girls, or here where my restless son
is handed a bow and shyly lifts a Douglas Cox violin,
the bow flaming in his first abraded minuet? In the barn, behind the shop,

it is lambing season. Jenny Girl has birthed three last night.
My son needs a boost to see over the rusted gate
the white lamb, the black lamb. The violin maker kneels over a third lamb
that lies too still. Jenny Girl stands thick-coated in the barn stall.

Vivaldi over and over watched his girls leave the music and go to men.
Coming off the hill, the wheels rump and spatter our windshield with mud.
My son says he knows the lamb is dead. Later, it's a matinee, the four-dollar
car wash, shrieking as straps come at us, monster perfect, slapping,

waxing, launching us mechanically through water, stalling in heat
until the aluminum arm lifts and we are sent out down another muddy road
where my son points to trees and sings scale notes of warning,
presage to the thickening violins who bud, ready for their orchestral bloom.

Three Twelve O'clocks in a Day

Somewhere late in the day's second night
I understand this fever does not care
if this is the very best boy,

the kind of boy who will not tell his friend
there are not three twelve o'clocks in a day
because he doesn't want to hurt her feelings.

And then I think that I am wrong
and just maybe the fever loves the boy,
loves possessively, loves him

extremely right up to one hundred and four where blistered,
his lips split into dry flaps
that will not soften when I sponge him down.

Maybe we are even alike,
the fever and the mother, both of us ready
to fight to the death for him.

Wasn't I trying to take down
the fever that was trying to knock out
an invisible germ?

But when it spikes one hundred and five point one
and this shivering boy whispers, "I'm sorry,"
when he can't stand to get to the toilet

or even sit up to vomit in the metal bowl,
then I know that if it loves anything at all,
the fever, it loves the burning,

and I see myself for the worn-out ranger that I am,
past thinking, just standing watching the blaze
with my leaky bucket and a spoon of sugar medicine,

surveying the razed, scorched land.
It is late. I am here breathing smoke.
Pray for a shift in the wind.

Such Noises

"I bet," a woman says, "this will show up in one of your fictions."

A man says, "Just don't ever tell them that."

"One day," he says, "I think you should write the story of how I gave her permission to kiss him."

She says, "You need to tell the one about the pigs they named after us."

And another time she says, "What about that teacher who wanted to talk about his great sex?"

She says, "Swear you'll never write this, but wouldn't it make a great story."

She says, "He didn't exactly piss in the linen drawer."

He says, "Please change the name of the woman."

He says, "That's not your story to tell,"

She says, "Don't forget that's my story." And the next day she calls to say, "You can have it. It's not the kind of story I'd ever want to tell."

He says, "A story of washing the body, tell me, wouldn't that be a good one?"

She says, "Can you please just leave that part out!"

He says, "She really wasn't like that."

She says, "What about a story about the girl and the brother?"

She says, "You've got to get in the part about after they'd butchered the pigs, they froze and labeled the parts, V's ribs, N's chops, V's feet, N's loin."

He says, "This is definitely going to show up in one of your stories."

She says, "How come you never write about me?"

He says, "No question about it, this is your kind of story, isn't it?"

"I bet," the woman says, "I just bet you'll get it wrong."

Altered Woman

The next morning the calculations she had made the night before seemed like odd scribbles, inconsequential, and so entirely wrong that she could not quite believe they were what she had ever actually written down. She tried to figure out where she might have come up with those specific calculations, but none of it fit any part of anything she could think of so that, as the morning wore on, she went back a few times to look them over, trying little by little to imagine what she might do, what alteration in demographics, marriage, food intake, for example, she might enact in her life to make that number come out right.

Intentional Woman

She is surprised, each time, that they say they like it when they first see her like that. She has taken steps, paid extra, buying non-reflective and ultra-thin that do not show just how much correction she actually needs. Still, it is not easy for her to walk out of the bathroom, to come up beside where this one stands at the window, or that one takes books off her bookshelves, and know that they will look up and see her this way. But here she is and he is saying, "I like you like that," and she does not like it, the way he looks now at her as if he is finally seeing the great secret of who she is. She does not like what she thinks he thinks her secret is, and she wants to tell him he is wrong, that she is more like whatever it was he saw before, though she can see he likes believing he is the only one who has seen her like this. He says, now, finally, she looks smart enough to own all these books. Then he kisses her as if he has always wanted to kiss a smart and bookish girl. Later she cannot find them on the shelf or on the floor or lost in the bedsheets and he says, "Let me help you look." and "I like when you need me to help you look." She does not like any of it. She tells him this. Eventually he remembers her as the one with bent frames that were always poking, pressing into his skin and getting in the way.

Measured Woman

A man did not want daughters. But was it as simple as that? —a not wanting?
—because, despite every medical, spiritual, and marital intervention, the man,
of course, had daughters. For one he seated the wife above him. For one he
spun down seed. He counted. He entered a trance. Microscopes measured the
wife's ferning. Daughter after daughter, six, to be exact, the man had, and, of
course, he loved the girls, wanting for each one of them all the same gorgeous,
wrong things he already wanted for the son.

Intact Woman

Because she finds it once in his closet, she begins looking for it all the time and comes to find that each month, just before the month ends, just like magic, there, in the closet, on top of the neat stack, is the new one. But she knows it is not magic, it is him, his doing, his handiwork. She wants to understand what is in it for him and because she feels she knows him, she feels she knows what in it particularly interests him, which pages do the trick—which is exactly what, this trick?—that is what she is trying to find out. She looks at the pages that she is certain get to him, and she tries to let them get to her, which she finds is easy enough, though she is not sure if that is because she is thinking that they— she and he—are both being gotten by the same thing or because she has now her own secret which is bigger than his secret because it includes his secret. She is surprised a little by how easy it is, an abracadabra, a one-two-three, and she is surprised, too, by how often she goes to his closet to be with him, though she understands her not being there is part of what is in it for him. But what if she is wrong? What if it is not the pages she thinks, but different ones, and when she thinks this she feels stupid and wrong and embarrassed and tricked by him. She is angry and feels he has forced her to go there. Then she is angry because she feels he has deserted her in their secret place. And then she remembers he does not know where she is, but she keeps it open just to what she thought was right for him because she is right in the middle of things, and she needs, all on her own, to finish up the dirty work.

Here Is Her Detailed List

The bonus word was wind.
She did not want Cairo.

And just forget, she announced, the Greycliff Ranch
where retarded twin teenage boys roamed the porch.

She demanded a stretch of arms,
a collarbone, chemicals.
Her requirements included gusts and breaches,
grazes of skin. Other words to include were fix and pin.
She refused to even consider either Rome or Utica.

She did not want the assured goddess
who takes frontage with someone who called
himself the Doctor of Secrets.
My God, she didn't have to be a genius
to see the Doctor of Secrets was not one to be trusted.
Still, out in Greycliff, there was no medicine or tall tales,
just one boy, all elbows and knees, rocking.
The other boy all just the same.

You must understand, a lady said,
we've got to keep those pesky things locked out of the house.

Please, whatever, not that!
—boys or secrets, the chemical stiff of cities.
Give her a detailed list of what she wanted.
Offer her a share in the endless incorporated.

But watch out! Here come boys,
buckle-legged off the porch with droopy, long-armed hugs.
She will have none of it.

Go ahead and try, but you can't fool her
with your collapsed coliseums, hydrogen shrines,
a snare of ladies nursing sons to oblivion.

Give her the bonus of wind.
Where was Utica? —she wondered, off some blowsy road?
—she would not go there! And Greycliff?
Who was trying to fool whom now? Those boys
beyond spelling bees—thank God.
They were another lady's worry. Still they loped toward her.

She might, after all, want the doctor, the pin and fix inside his bag.

Then she'd see those details stumble off, righteously,
like sullen teenagers pulling at themselves forever.

She might, after morning, put nothing on her list.

Standing Woman

He says, "Look!" and then when she looks up at him, he says, "Oh, no!" because she has stepped on the joined, red dragonflies he wanted her to look at on the rutted, grown-over car path up from the beach. She starts to say, "It's okay," she thinks she's really just grazed them with the side of her foot, but he says, "No," picks up the red dragonflies and says, "Look. They're squashed." Then she feels big and oafish and tries making a little joke, "Well, that was some ménage à trois. I hope, at least, they felt something." He starts to say something and stops. He is quiet on the rest of their walk and quiet through the lunch they eat standing together at the sink, or later, when she stings him with her mouth and he starts to say, "No!" but she stops him with her mouth again, this time so soft he thinks of the frill of Queen Anne's Lace on another beach road with another woman who dared him to go ahead and look at the flower's center drop of blood.

Tilted Woman

Does it really matter, really, if it's true or not,
but just, really, to think of it, Tony Bennett's cock
in his hotel room at the San Juan Americana
while Rosario knelt over it, her mouth brushing over it,
her crooning, "Ladies and Gentlemen,
here tonight, straight from six-sold-out weeks
at the fabulous, the world famous Atlantic City's Taj Mahal
is the one, the only, Mister Tony Bennett."
And with that she'd sing, tilting and leaning into
the purpled head, all the old Tony Bennett classics
and for an encore some new songs
she'd make up for him on the spot.
What if it is true, really? What if I told you Rosario is a twin—
would that stretch your belief?
That they dance flamenco in separate cities?
That they are over fifty? That the sister's name means hope?
Are you with me still? Are you really ready to know
that all Tony Bennett wanted was to go down on her,
that she claims that after coming
her mouth goes cold as marble? She has lost me
with this intrusion of limestone, and I refuse to lose you.
It's just her claim, after all. I have heard a woman claim
that she didn't like it, a man's mouth on her,
or women who will not take a man in their mouths,
let alone to sing the cock, sing the cock,

and other women, still, exhausted by claims.
I want none of it, I want it all, your castanet heart,
your secrets walking around naked, a rash of honesty,
your raucous coming, not stilled. Does the twin's mouth
marble too? The San Juan Americana, that sounds
good enough to me. And for you, can we say love?
Can we say he went there thirsting her ochreous menses
and came up smeary and beyond any backyard God.
Tell me, really, Tony, is it true— ochred or purpled
or San Juan? How are the new classics?
In the next suite there is always a man on a phone
claiming, "I'm just the same in real life."
In the next to the next room, room service knocks twice.
The hotel charges fifty cents a call. *Can we say love?*
"Is that what you wanted?" he said. Plates and forks,
eggs and meat ransacked on the tray outside the door.
"Not till you went there," she said, "Now it's all I want."

Prior Woman

My mother says she has been in Switzerland at a fabulous spa when she shows up in my dream, and I say, "Switzerland? I thought you were dead." She laughs and says, "Not the last time I looked," and strikes a pose, looking so fabulous and so alive and so young like the photographs of her from before I was born. I hold her face to kiss her, but when I touch her she begins to shred, and soon she is in strips and pieces stuck on my lips and hands.

Recorded Woman

Once I taught in a town where I could not look at the faces the boys and girls
were stuck with, like acres of bad land to farm from the get go, all rut and
steep pock hill, damn holes thick with bees so that to plant each year the soil
stung to touch.

It is dumb to say it hurt to teach them, their turned-in eyes, dull looks I could
not bear, so I busted their heads down in books, till they got their grades and
tore to the edge of town where soon they were the dads' bent faces split over
two beers and a shot.

It hurt to get food in stores where I did not want to look up at the bred-wrong
moms so I spoke down to shoes and carts of shit food, corn in cans, and fish in
a box.

Each night I'd shut the school and climb the back of a bald rock hill. I saw out
through a pink sky to where the town lights snapped, one by one the small
homes lit. In gold light I watched their bad heads bowed over bad food. The
boys and girls buzzed like yard sparks. It hurt to see such gut, homely love. I
thought they were fields, bum crops that should be cut and burned.

Once who the fuck was I? What hell did my ugly heart know?

Unnamed Woman

His not-yet-ex-wife has taken home some 15-year-old's week-old baby from a hospital in Bozeman. Holding him tonight, I feel her rise to the rasping 3 A.M. hunger of this still-unnamed girl baby. I would go to her, show her what little I know to do—hoist a baby up on a shoulder to force out crampy gas. And I would go to the 15-year-old child, dab a warm cloth along her stitched perineum.

Our lives are strange. That's the easy thing to say. He curls deeper into me, this man who noises to the lightest touch, this man who wakes and leaves by five so that when my boys drift to my bed they find me alone waiting to soothe them back to sleep.

Judge none of us the debt of happiness we impose on each other. Judge not the eggs stained by age or heat. Judge not this man and his still-wife, mother now to a child born of a child in a state where I have never slept. I am not sleeping now. I am a worry of names. I am a whisper of cooled chamomile to ease colic. I am rampant with life for all its strange desire. I am feet astride this man, dancing him awake.

I am not telling you how to live. He pulls me to him. Let there be wind or no wind. There is no easy way to fly.

Cut Woman

When I call Nance at her mother's house and she says she's going over to our
old town pool because Jack O'Hara died on the exploded July 22 TWA Flight
800 to Paris, I think, for a second, she is saying Frank O'Hara—who, trust me,
Nance has never heard of—has died but no, it is Jack O'Hara, that kid, the
diving pool lifeguard she spent a summer, 21 years ago, jumping in a yellow
bikini off the high board for, and by about this time in July they were sneaking
back at night to skinny-dip and mess around on the mowed town slope, though
it was over by the end of August when Nance and I cracked eggs on his front
steps and muttered into phones, "This one's for Jack." But today she's 38 and
jumping and Jack has living 12-year-old twin boys and Nance, oddly, has
twins, too, a boy and girl who so herniated and stretched her skin that she will
not wear bikinis even after the repair surgery which has to be checked tomor-
row so she needs to change our plans she tells me when I call, which is okay by
me because I was in no rush to drive out of the city and because, as Frank said,
　　　"and the world holds its breath
　　　　　to see if you are there, and safe
　　　　　　　are you?"

Noisy Woman

If at least this one beautiful day isn't all hers, then who is that old Jew of her soul limping through the passenger terminal?

She's the first to kvell over anything that sparkles.

It is not without sadness that she loves the dogwood. See, she wears the badge of a citizen pruner. Beware, when she takes her axe to the limbs, there will be no hesitation.

Get on!

She'll take her three chances, no more refugee child in a split-level ranch apologizing for her no-good-easy-luck. She adores the glossy vanity of yard tulips.

Just leave her pity at the boatyard playing its chipped ocarina. She has glasses thick enough to see how the nasty swans ruffle and hiss at her song.

Living Woman

The tumors are beautiful, the doctors say, encased like two eggs sealed in a plastic baggie. She must feel more than hopeful, she must feel good, they insist, really, only two tumors—twins, like her own boy and girl.

So that weeks later, after the third radiation, after the prednisone keeps her up all night, she is in the kitchen packing lunches when a twinge, a break of nausea rashes across her, she holds, steady, hands flat against the counter,

thinks, "Morning sickness. I remember this. This means life."

The Vow

Across the city you enter me.   A wind hurries to keep up.   There is no
keeping up.

Everything in the city holds a palm out.   Between us, we use everything.
There, here, and again.

Notes

"The Bounty" is dedicated to Gerald Stern.

"Bright Hill" is dedicated to Sonya Del Peral.

"Unnamed Woman": The final line in this poem is gratefully borrowed and adapted from "Sugar on the Floor," written by Kiki Dee and sung by Etta James on *Etta James Live from San Francisco.*

"Cut Woman": The final lines are quoted from Frank O'Hara's closing lines from the poem "Ode to Tanaquil Leclercq."

"Noisy Woman": "Kvell" is a Yiddish word; it roughly translates as to gush or boast with pleasurable abandon.

"Living Woman" is dedicated to Nancy Rockland-Miller.